The Salty River Bleeds

poems by

Stephen Page

Finishing Line Press
Georgetown, Kentucky

The Salty River Bleeds

Copyright © 2019 by Stephen Page
ISBN 978-1-64662-025-8 First Edition
All rights reserved under International and Pan-American Copyright Conventions.
No part of this book may be reproduced in any manner whatsoever without written
permission from the publisher, except in the case of brief quotations embodied in
critical articles and reviews.

ACKNOWLEDGMENTS

Publisher: Leah Maines

Editor: Christen Kincaid

Cover Art: William E Brill, artist

Author Photo: Lidia Papaleo and digitally enhanced by Multiple Michael.

Cover Design: Elizabeth Maines McCleavy

Printed in the USA on acid-free paper.
Order online: www.finishinglinepress.com
           also available on amazon.com

           Author inquiries and mail orders:
               Finishing Line Press
                 P. O. Box 1626
            Georgetown, Kentucky 40324
                   U. S. A.

Table of Contents

Proem A 1
Jonathan Goes to Search for It at Sunset 2
Finally 3
Muse in Different Forms 4
Fauna 5
Dear Nephew 6
Dear Father 7
Cattle Rustler 9
Horse Thief 11
Bad Guy Caught Red-Handed 12
Tattler 13
His Name is Pac-Man 14
On a Breath-Mist Morning 15
Last Night I Dreamed Rain 16
Bad Guy Remains Unashamed 17
The Ranch Manager Thinking in His Office While Cleaning
   His Shotgun 18
On Ranching 20
The Wayward 21
Casca and Tattler 22
Tattler's Reindoctrination 23
Satellites 24
Punch Clock 26
The King of Clear 27
Tattler Too, ... 28
Misionero 30
Excuse Maker 31
The Legend of Wood 32
Ally, aka Advisor, Resigns 33
Philanderer 35
The Warning 36
Central Home 37
The Complexity of Managing Ranch Employees 38
The Cycle of Things on Santa Ana and Everywhere 39
What a Father Wants to Say to His Son 40
It Never Ends 41
In the Local News 43
Another Week Begins 45
Parrot Plague 46
While Watching TV After Hunting Opossum all Night 47
The Head 48
In the Room of the Dead 50

Damien Ricardo III and Goneril Elektra 52
Let the White Pills, ... 54
Morning Routines 55
His Nightly Bottle of Wine 56
Communication with the Capataz 58
Place for the Pueblo Teacher 60
The Language Teacher 61
Your Violet Hair Ribbon 62
Teresa: My Mask of Day 63
Teresa: Translator 64
On a Winter Walk 66
Transition 67
The Salty River 68

Ennui - Old Man 69

Glossary and References I 71

Dedicated to Old Man

This is a story of Jonathan and his wife Teresa, eco-ranchers.

All events, characters, and places in these poems are fictitious. Any resemblance to real events, real people, or real places is coincidental.

Epigraphs

"I is not me."
—Baudelaire

"To understand one, is to better understand the other. To understand one, is to understand the One."
—SMP

"When we lose our myths, we lose our place in the universe."
—Madeleine L'Engle

"A human being is a part of the whole called by us 'universe,' a part limited in time and space. He experiences himself, his thoughts and feelings as something separated from the rest, a kind of optical delusion of his consciousness. This delusion is a kind of prison for us, restricting us to our personal desires and to affection for a few persons nearest to us. Our task must be to free ourselves from this prison by widening our circle of compassion to embrace all living creatures and the whole of nature in its beauty."
—Albert Einstein

"The clearest way into the Universe is through a forest wilderness."
—John Muir

"Look deep into nature, and then you will understand everything better."
—Albert Einstein

"In every walk with nature one receives far more than he seeks."
—John Muir

"All trees need a voice."
—Aubrey Arch

"Be sure you put your feet in the right place, then stand firm."
—Abraham Lincoln

"If you want me again look for me under your boot-soles."
—Walt Whitman

"Truth, crushed to earth, will rise again."
—Dr. Martin Luther King. Jr.

Proem

Obligation is inside *Santa Ana's* main *tranquera*.

His hair is black, as are his eyes, beard, suit, and tie.

He holds a folded newspaper under his arm.

He smiles at the Beauty of Ranch.

Jonathan Goes to Search for It at Sunset

An owl screeches from the oven.
A ratbird skittles across the windowsill.

Monarchs fill a white afternoon.
A cow walks in front of the sun.

Cut grass rolls toward the barn,
horseless as he passes it toward Wood

carrying a backpack with *mate,* a snack,
binoculars, a flashlight, a notebook, a pen.

As his tired feet pass Horse Lot,
the hot air will not fill his lungs.

The meat and cheese Teresa prepared
leads two collies and hairy horse flies.

Once again he is left standing
some hundreds of meters from Wood,

because he finds his pants are much too thin
to cross the lots with thistle.

The Myth he searches for must certainly be there,
in puddles swimming with tadpoles and larvae,

in crepuscular knitting together the trees,
in lightning bug flashes and cricket chirps.

Finally

While it is yet dark I slide from between
the sheets, pad to the kitchen, brew coffee,
and pack *facturas* in a plastic bag. I strip
off my pajamas, shower myself with insect
repellent, and put on yesterday's clothes. I
shoulder my backpack, and slip out the back
door, closing it quietly behind me. In the vestige
of moonlight I walk past the barn, feeling the dew
wet my ankles. Just inside the edge of
Wood I breakfast on a tree stump. Two barn
owls screech at my invasion and leave their
branch perch. A bat flaps violently by my
head. I roll marmalade around my tongue
and smell fecund earth spiced with decaying
leaves. A silver fox darts across a clearing,
and I unseat myself to wander Wood.
In the penumbrae of trees I walk—I listen to
silence—I do not feel the weight of my
pack—I misplace time—an hour when I click
the light on my digital watch. The Myth
I seek does not appear, but I feel I was close
to finding it, or it finding me. A wood dove pops
its wings as it departs eucalypti mist auraed by
a vanilla sunrise. Tree-frog croaks crescendo
then stop as I exit the treeline. A peach sun rises
behind a windmill as I cross the field to breakfast
a second time, this time with Teresa.

In a lemon tree behind our ranch house, I discover
a newly made wasp nest bowing a brace of branches.

Muse in Different Forms

I see you walking through Wood,
though your image is ephemeral:
yellow eyes and blood-blonde hair,
linen robe and leather sandals dissolve
as I enter the treeline then solve as suns.

One day as Teresa and I drive through
Santa Ana's gates, we see Old Man
shimmering upon the dirt road wearing
a tattered coat. As we approach him,
his unshaven face and he disappear.

Why does Black Dog always
follow me when I go on my strolls,
my Wood walks, my Myth finding;
Why does he shadow away the finches
that silhouette their evergreen theater?

I sit in my *matera* in the heat
of January while a luteous *chimango*
worms the grass outside my window.

Once I freed two caged owls
that flew up into a moonless sky.

Fauna

Fauna is absent from Wood of late,
I cannot see her from my tree stump—
She has lit to trees and burrowed underground
Escaping the face of four-legged Helios.

Cynthia came to me in my tower—
She wore a diadem and sheer short robe
And while I lay naked on my carpet
She straddled me with her sandal-strapped calves.

Rosemary outside my *matera* window
Scents the sough of Delphi's cloud
Buzzed northerly by the bumblebee
Brandishing his long red clover tongue.

Diana was once a lover of mine
That flew with me to California
And shotgunned in my rusty Volkswagen
But did not vacate my New York studio.

After four long years of living with Helen
And never touching barefoot Delos
Artemis leaned over fresh cut grass
With sunburnt face and parchment lips.

Dear Nephew,

Today you are twenty-three. The same age I was when I joined the Marines.

Your mother tells me you are having some problems with finances, with organizing your life—that you want to join the Marines.

I remember well when you were not twenty-three, before I was, and when I was, even a little after. One day, when you were just a kid, we had to go pick up my father's car in the middle of a blizzard. Well, the snow was already three feet deep, and you and I . . .

Oh, I have to leave off for now. Have to go. You know how it is, now that you are an adult. Work. The *Capataz* just called me on the radio. He calls me *Don*, or *Señor*. A cow is dead. I have to go see it. More on the car adventure later. You must visit me on the ranch. I have taken over as ranch manager due to some administrative and personnel problems. I did not ask for this job, I liked teaching, but life takes you into some unplanned territory sometimes . . .

Have to go. Take care. Be strong.

Your Uncle,

Jonathan

PS Don't worry that you have no order, no discipline. That will follow with your place.

PPS I am sure that everyone is always telling you who you are, what you will be. I heard them when I was there, when you were there, when I was there and you were not there. Be where you want to be.

Dear Father,

I am so pleased that you have volunteered for Meals on Wheels—a noble endeavor to say the least. The driving around and handing out of containered food must surely keep you busy, which as we both know is something you need to do, especially now, at this point in your life.

Here on *Santa Ana* it is raining, a necessity for all ranches and farms alike. There always seems to be too much or too little of the wet stuff: cows either grazing in knee-deep water or chewing cud in puddles of dust, wheat like reeds in lakes, or corn withering and dropping cracked ears. Last week the soy leaves turned from yellow to brown, a worsening state of bad, and the windbreak evergreens ochred the cow-lot borders. This afternoon, after two hours of steady raindrops the size of acorns, the whole ranch and everything on it seemed to sigh with relief, an almost audible sigh like one you hear in a dream as you are waking. The land has blackened to chocolate and the air chilled to jacket weather. Today's downpour reprieved a two-month bout of ninety-degree swelter that made ill the character of the entire *Santa Ana* populace, not to mention tainted much of our cupboard tins and racked red wine.

We start the *yerra* next week—a picnic for us, as we watch while the *gauchos* perform. The cooler weather will be perfect for it. In a month or so we sell the calves.

I am sure you are happy that you will soon move to Florida after such a cold Michigan winter. Two months of breath-cracking, below-zero temperatures are enough to make anyone seek guayaberas and daiquiris on the beach. Retirement will be pure pleasure. No more up before daybreak! No more "thru rain and shine!"

I hope your recovery from prostate surgery goes well. A hobby is in order for you to find, as we spoke about, to keep you occupied. Distracted. Don't be like your father. Your career is over, not your life.

I trust this letter finds you and Mom well.

With much thought,

Your son, Jonathan

PS The jacket you gave me during my last visit, the bombardier with the shoulder insignia missing, keeps me from the wet and chill. I use it on my Wood walks.

Cattle Rustler

When Teresa and I arrived on the ranch
in my 4 by 4
you smiled and waved from Red House porch,
then you scowled and glared
when we piled out
and you noticed we had with us
the *pueblo's escribiano,* and Advisor.
We asked you to bring to the corral
the eleven extra calves Tattler told us you had
in Lot Ten.

In the shade of the trees next to the chute,
you glared at us and unsheathed
your silver *facón* and sharpened it,
then shaved a calf's hindquarter
looking for the brand
you knew was not there.
You were calm and meticulous in your shaving,
but when Notary whispered to Advisor
that that the calf and the other ten
were much fatter than the rest of the calves on the ranch,
you jerked your hand,
slicing the calf's flank, cutting off
any denial.

"Three," you said "three," with fingers
upheld, "three" is all the animals you lost
in the history of your work. But what about the extras—
the Eleven here in the corral?

They had to be trucked to the neighbor's ranch,
where the owner employed Accomplice Two.

For four days Teresa, Advisor, and I
listened as you denied, confessed,
denied, confessed, cried,
and more-than-once sharpened

your *facón* in front of us.

Your renouncement was only signed
when Teresa waved her hand and said,
"Enough, enough bloodshed. We gave
you our trust, which you stabbed then twisted
into my pelvis, which will never again birth
confidence in your bull-brown eyes."

Horse Thief

You left on vacation the day we threw Rustler
off the ranch, your taillights brandishing out
the front gates, and for ten days peace settled
upon the ranch, the mockingbirds nestling inside
the casco, the cows cudding, the bulls feeding
in Lot Ten, even the sheep not baa-ing, and except
for two of your mongrels loosing themselves from
their tethers and breaking into the henhouse, the sun settled
red and rose yellow; even the weekend rain pithed softly
into the soil, regreening by Monday the dormant
winter grass.

You are Accomplice, the one who Tattler told us
helped Rustler, the one who lives near the back gate,
the one who sleeps all day and nightly visits the neighbor
riding roan horses that ghost the plains.

A thunderstorm rivered the road on the night of your
return, preventing you from driving out the main
gate at your leisure, and when we locked the back
gate, you were disallowed cowardly exit. The new working
hours I set confined your family's laughter to
your kitchen, which, by the second day was locked inside
a corner cupboard, becoming cobweb. You stood outside
my *casco* at predawn and belligerently questioned
my order of the day, unhorsing you. You threatened
to quit, which I granted permission, which pressed
your lips together and skulked you toward the firewood
piled next to the barn, where you picked up an ax,
sharpened it as you glared at me, then turned
and stared beyond your unsaddled horse
at the new calves watching you from within
the *Santa Ana* fenceline.

Bad Guy Caught Red-Handed

Your brilliant black boots and gold-inlaid silver *rastra* shone through the white of your newly washed pickup laden low with sheep hides. You are so transparent. How long did you take to shine those boots yet wet with spit? And what fine leather they are. *Ternero* hide? *Cordero* skin? How long did you take to flay those sheep whose skins lie so limply wet in your truck? And how the hell could you afford a gold-inlaid silver *rastra*?

Some months ago your phone decided
not to lift or ring,
so you could not report morning births,
and I could not question nightly deaths.

What do you mean I have no right to ask what is your business? Your business? Your business is to work for the salary we pay. And those sheep hides? They are from your sheep, not mine. And these hours? These are the hours you work for us. What do you mean I do not trust you to work eight hours when I just last week found you rounding up newly calved cows and herding them behind your house in the middle of the morning to milk and make cheese to sell during our working hours?

In three weeks you consumed a cow,
murdered another,
assassinated a calf, but
their blood does not brown the grass.

You think while looking through your close-set mercury eyes that my admin is uncountable and the two-hour curving highway between us will horse you time to town.

I braided a noose out of calf hide,
carry a nine-millimeter on my hip,
constructed a yardarm outside my office,
and am at my desk, sharpening my belt-knife.

Tattler

Your tale is told.
Tell it again

Without your telling
Told again.

After Rustler and Horse Thief stopped losing head in Lot Eight, clover-fat calves ate hunter free, but horse-shook cows exploded with gas. Your unmean mien and can-do smile electrified paddocks in twos and threes. Summer sun unwatered tanks, and mismanaged grass capitulates capacity. The fence that sent Hobble Foot on bike, broke this week under hungry cow weight. The chickens that laid, lay no more, while uncounted lambs grill on Sunday. Your salary arrived late today, so your rubber check melts in your pocket. Rancid Post Maker humbly sat, wringing his hat in his lap. Unscented fertilizer that you bagged, stacked like shit under the barn. You think inchoately to spread by word, something developed sometime before, by Silent Mechanic and Talkative Salesman, drinking *mate* under Octagon Shed.

His Name is Pac-Man

He is Man of War, a king in his own world,
a roan with a forehead mark of white whale
and fetlocks that beard nobly. He grazes
where he pleases, when he pleases. He
is ridden by whom he chooses. He is saddled
by King. He carries King who rides
herniated and allows him free graze.
He shakes his armor off to let his pelt
breathe. He makes summer sun spring,
and leaps fences in search of rain.
He cuts cattle and runs errands
for *Don*. He unhinges barn
doors and watches stars crystallize new
leaf dew hooved by the remaining five
broken horses that do not follow
him. The moon haloes his mane
as he learns the phases of grass.
After months of war, he has found place.
The Five now follow and beg permission
to move. He has found life in the vision
of ranch, and eats it voraciously.

On a Breath-Mist Morning

The Gauchos and I were on *recorrido*, our twenty hooves dragging arbitrary lines through the frost, the horses snorting and neighing, occasionally farting. A red Hereford stood heavy and alone in the middle of a field with hind legs spread, her eyes wet, when suddenly, she lifted her tail and one embryonic pink hoof poked out of her uterus to the shin then stopped, protruding like a hard branch. The cow bawled. Tattler injected her with dilator, and dark-eyed Accomplice guided her from paddock three to the corral, where he lassoed her, tied her back legs together, wrestled her to the ground, and roped her front legs to her neck. He slipped one olive hand into the uterus and extracted another hoof, looped soft white cord around the two limbs, then, standing alongside nervous-eyed Tattler, grasped the long ends of the cord and tugged, tugged, tugged…tugged until the head plopped out. The mother was untied and the afterbirth slopped into a steamy pile upon the ground; and she, freed from the mass of birth yet unable to stand, raised her head and glanced up at each of us, the three of us, as we stood over her, then strained her neck in order to see over her belly and hip, stared at her calf until breath raised its ribs.

Last Night I Dreamed Rain

The clouds quickened under a wax
moon, then settled around plastic palm
fronds. My truck stuck in riverbed
three, and just like the time it slipped
into a ditch, I tried to push it out
alone, putting it in gear, then straining
under the bumper, only this time Tale
Teller arrived on our tractor without my call.
Voiceless, I accepted his pull, the Fence
Builders "heying" from a distance. Damp Cat
rubbed my bare legs while I smoked
a filterless cigarette and Blonde Collie Bitch chased
white ponies around the yard. A blue-eyed
blonde woman, her hair plastered
to her face, her freckles sheening, a scotch
on the rocks in her hand, offered me a blow
job while I barbequed blood
sausage and tenderloin. A pebble-sized
coal, meant to sizzle the meat, rolled
off the brick platform and plopped
into the sand, burrowed under my shoe and came
to rest against the dry grass edging the lawn.
I poured out half a cold beer to extinguish the flames,
and then it began to rain.

Bad Guy Remains Unashamed

The four calves were penned in a tight corral
behind the boarding building where Fat Pig
resided under your office desk cluttered with
instruments of ambivalent usage and the butcher
room sparkled with an all-too-recent hose down.

Soon-to-be-Retired offered us *mate*
inside his Spartan two-room abode but could not
testify to your possession of extra animals
because he was always forbidden entry into your yard
and knew only that the neighbor locked the gate.

Your sheep are eating all the cow grass
while your butter churner robs your saddle
hours and your Irish princess with soft cheeks
looks in the mirror at her black eye
and your skinned knuckles gripping her shoulder.

You sat in the kitchen drinking grappa while sharpening your *facón*
with your front door slightly ajar
while Teresa and I drove by without waving
not failing to notice your teenage daughter
standing on the porch with her arm in a sling.

The Ranch Manager Thinking in His Office While Cleaning His Shotgun

Your breath is marked,
blackness veins its cloud
like a smoker's x-ray.

And you, whose daughters whom
I sacrifice my Sunday
sleep-ins for; you who I drove
to hospital twice, once to slice
out an ovary, and once to scrape
out a lifeless fetus embedded
in your uterus wall; you,
who do not anoint
your mother's ring finger.

Your green-eyed wife serves lemon cake
on blue china
while silver stirrups adorn your walls.

You, who hobbling arrive
upon deboned pastures
soon after my lighter flicked
out the crimson palms
of the olive Horse Thief. You,
who refusing to autograph
machete and ax, putter upon a rusty moped
exiting the white gates.

Your kitchen fires are all extinguished
and neighbors bleach
the sooty tiles.

You, who point
a self-righteous finger
fattened with law,
immediately impregnate
one tulip; you, who
came second, pin

a prophylactic; you
who signed a prenup
and run my horse to foam.

You who put to seed
our best cattle; you,
who picked their lice
and planted them
in ever concentric
furrows; you, who left
the fenceline open
all weekend.

You, you all, you nine in a line,
will never again breathe
my air.

All your separation papers
are stacked neatly
upon my metal desk.

On Ranching

All this ass kicking and horse riding
and calf pulling and gate lifting and truck
pushing has herniated my abdomen.
*The fleeting rain does not puddle as
it did last month.* Constants are
falling fenceline and the need
for grass. *I have been here before.
I have been here before.* The new
gaucho enters my office for the first
time, and I have seen his face
somewhere. *Here.* His black sombrero,
bombachas, and silver spurs; his white beach
hat, blue jeans, and tennis shoes. *Again, again.*
the mail lady's red hair keeps me supplied
with stamps. *Me Tarzan, you Jane.*
A rice shoot leans against my desk
lamp, and outside, wheat is shin
high. *Cut the thistle, cut the thistle.*
The security chain we had for months
on gate twenty-eight can be slipped
right over the post.
*Have you ever had brain cells zapped
by an electric fence?* The Cultivators
are fumigating again. *A beetle falls
upon my notebook.* I must keep
the calves from vaginal death,
and the cows from exploding with bloat.

The Wayward

Cows spilled out onto a moonless road,
and the white truck parked itself in front
of your home. Your scarlet jacket drapes
its seat. The tractor would not move and dug
itself deeper into mud. Fence posts raced
a thousand meters, then walked back, losing
line. The coffeed nightmares night not rain
but pen unplanned plans on paper. My saddle you
horse and barbwire yours, the nails unstucking
crude leather. My salty lasso you snapped
in two, cat-o-nining your shoulders and
back. The leather rack must be lifted
to shade, its sunned stench
olfactoring office windows. Electrify
Lot Sixteen, and fatten uncorned cows.
Lot Ten's drainage ditch caves in
both sides of the road and snakes
replicate unwooded cement worm
tubes. Cereal Man pushed our combined
road further onto my property,
and while you slept, I went
wading into the wheat, searching
for the cows that were not there.

Casca and Tattler

I long ago put on my battle gear,
And now it is hard to take it off.

I run across pastures with my sword
Raised, looking for someone to decapitate.

After you tattled the tale of Horse Thief,
Your saddled numbers did not mesh,

And after we fired Cattle Rustler
Your calving measures shortened.

Why do you have a premade excuse
For every task incomplete;

Why can't you finish cutting the lawn,
or completely paint the barn;

Why are the pastures not divided,
And the cows passing through canals?

I sliced your tongue off in mid-sentence
And ripped your lips from your cheeks,

And yet you have the tears to rust
The talisman from my armor.

The King/I are a lot like
Macbeth standing over the servants:

"Who do I have to report to now,
When my position is uncertain?"

How do you change from war to life:
Do you just let things go?

Maybe they should stop giving medals:
Look what happened to Douglas MacArthur.

Tattler's Reindoctrination

In our hebdomadal meetings I will teach you
how to nail a cadaver to a count post:
through the eye socket picked clean by vultures;

How to blue-bread mold tuberculars,
and chart them for Horseback Vet;
How to lift cement blocks with one finger,

Burn urea bags after it rains,
Sell soy seed at a corn bazaar,
Hang hunters by their watch chains.

Every day I work with you
I find less that you want to learn:
I need to return to my teaching.

You tire me. I wish not to see you;
I wish to call you long distance,
The wires sparkling platinum with current.

Do not touch the wires, learn that they are there,
Learn to walk within electric-fenced lots,
Learn that eucalypti prevent sun stroke.

Lift your scarlet jacket from the barn door;
Do not write "pickup security tour,"
Instead of "Sunday afternoon trip to town."

Satellites

The tree frogs called the rain last night,
but the rain did not answer.
The intermittent croaking, about
every hour or so, was followed by
a gust of wind and the scent
of water, but no sprinkle, no pour.

The new *gaucho*, angelic Moral
who rides our horse to sores,
has dried the soy beans not yet
planted. He horns the sun and peels
paint from his home.

Twenty millimeters of rain is not
forty nine, even with the north
wind. Two plastic gauges announce
the Tattler's arrival in the *casco*.

The newer *gaucho*, taller, broader
shouldered than Angel
shunned away, suffers the sun
of unshaded Twenty-One with
a smile and shovel-blistered hands
(but later became Excuse Maker).

Just one day of computer-
promised rain should soften the earth
and shoot the canal
full of internet cable, that is,
if the flexible orange pipe is found
on time.

With each truck that passes Lot
Three, earth crumbles and narrows
the road. We hope that the Three
barricade that which blackened
and thinned the cows.

I will the odometer to quit
increasing exponentially, and the bushes
Teresa planted to not yellow near
our home.

Punch Clock

Tattler, Tattler, quit telling
your tale; I arrive and find you
in your lounging pants, your horse
unsaddled. Quit looking bleary-eyed
at me and saying you arrived just
five minutes ago. Quit. Quit.

The Bug Sprayers inject their venom
into the air, multi streams of DDM
needle outward like an inside-out
Iron Maiden; the entrapped: cows,
birds, butterflies; the punished:
you and I; the ruined: global atmosphere,
water supplies; the victims: the unfed
of the earth told lies of quick
profit and promise of a new grain belt.

You who weigh the wheat honestly,
step off the scale "To see my father
in the hospital," then park your pickup
in front of the couple-hotel while
your wife measures fish portions
for the children at home: I should
believe your numbered cards?

The ants are carnivorous here
where I wait for the wheat to be cut:
From the furrows of your lies
they attack my legs; the three-day dead
cow is bones picked clean; red welts
painfully lifting my skin organ, the ribs
a cage of death stink; why did
I park here? Is this really the cow you claim?

Another sixteen-hour workshift, another
no-life dinner alone. Three days
is but a little, even for the vultures
perched on the fenceline, their sclerae red.

The King of Clear

Tell Post Maker to stop cutting trees, because
I will never bequeath thin-shelled bird eggs, mud
slides, baked rain.

Now chickens are where the pigs should
not be, and Emerald Room smells cleanly
of leather. Your sheep hides are salted
in the transit room, and another cow
that roamed my *Pampa* has passed
through your gullet. Stop being a *gaucho*
and start being a gaucho: fix the fence,
repair the water mill, cut the thistle,
count the head correctly, hop down
from your horse and work, stop
sleeping in the afternoon and slaughtering
my nights; and you, you who advise
land management, read history, learn
how mass agriculture changes weather patterns—
You will never have Lot Eight, You
Will never have Lot Eight, You will
Never have Lot Eight, You will never
Have Lot Eight, You will never have
Lot Eight, You will never have Lot
Eight, You will never have Lot Eight;
sooner or later, your cow-blood hands
will see light, even if you scrub them
in the stagnate trough under the broken mill.

Tattler Too,

You have left, the last of the liars and thieves.
I am still here.
My armor is intact.
I had reason to keep it on.

I have learned to lie and I don't like it.
Policy, politics, public relations,
A smile with a frown concealed,
A handshake with a dagger palmed.

You left like a thief in the night,
A raper, a burglar, a husband with a guilty
Conscience. I did not try to take your pen,
I paid you what you were worth,
I only drove your sister to town
So she could see the sights.

I am missing five cows, a horse,
A standing closet, a truck battery,
A solar panel, a tire jack, accounts.

My promise of a better home for you
Will construct this month, the Architects
Are at the gate, their tools in hand,
Their trucks laden with wood beams
And cement, floor tiles, window frames.

I never invaded your home without permission,
Never spoke to your sister behind the barn.
You tipped the scales, opened the gates,
Divided the calves by sex.

Your broken middle finger will never heal
Because your window keeps slamming shut upon it.
Now it is locked. Drive, drive your truck handcuffed
To the wheel, blind yourself with headlights.

Your wife abandoned you when she found out
You took bribes and that Whistling *Gaucho* was fired, for he
Visited her in the afternoons while you were
On the other side of the *estancia*, lining your pockets
With soy seed.

Misionero

On the patio, the cat waits,
meows, waits. She only comes when
the Architects are not reconstructing
Red House that Tattler thought
was for him. Blonde Collie Bitch
lies in heat upon the lawn. She hides
from Black Bastard Sunday.
Capataz's house is empty,
and cold. It no longer electrifies
the fence that separates the Bulls
from the Cows. Excuse Maker
has returned and partially corrupted
Misionero, who with his blue
poncho to fend off cold, walks through
the predawn dew in quest of the horse
that can be ridden but is not yet broke.

Misionero counts cows and gives
change. His river-black hair and brown
eyes lure the Cows to calve and
Palomino to pony. He must vacate
Transit House and live
in Central Home without lights.

Excuse Maker

The tractor was broke
The radio wasn't working
I didn't have time
I was sick that day
It was raining
The fence line was under water
The days are too long
The calves are being born now
The cows have screw worms
The horses have parasites
The horses are tired.

There is always a reason
for not completing a task,
but the tractor works when
you need it to haul firewood
to your hearth. You are healthy
on the weekends, and gone, the wild
horses you don't want to break.

You are Saboteur, Silent Tractor
Mechanic, you quit when Tattler belittled
you, but returned after he was fired, saying
he was in the wrong. Now you mope, stumble,
ride around caped in black. You spread disease,
plague, encephalitis, Red Death.
Maybe Tattler told a dark truth.

This hot spring afternoon I removed a vaccination
from the fridge. I immunized the other
employees. You, I will cure, or eradicate.
You will not epidemic the endemic.

At least you are not ingratiative
like Tattler, though I know
you have a silver-fox face. You
may run the canals at night,
but I see you, in the moonlight.

The Legend of Wood

We all have our stories to tell.
The weak and the strong, the rich
And the poor, the old and the young.
Which story do you have to tell, and
From which point-of-view do you wish to person?

Losing water from the beauty of river bank
The One appears in a world
Of blindness traversed by feeling
The leaves on corn plants and following
The rows, then stumbling through bean plants,
And wading through wheat.

The shore beats me to the Salty River
And spills its angled plots of produce
Into the muck of eoned knowledge.
I race like a cloud to see everything
And forget that I am only dissipating.

She waits under the sheet of night,
Upon the bank of the river,
Lying among the reeds,
Naked, wet with sweat, asleep,
Fingernails combing her pubes,
My name upon her lips, the tip
Of her tongue tapping the 't'
After the serpent hiss of 's',
The shudder releasing her dream.

Her names are Legend of Wood,
Lady of Violets;
Her names soon to be forgotten.

Ally, aka Advisor, Resigns

You have exchanged the blue coat we gave you
For a red one; or is it just reversible?

Don't snarl at me, you are not a lion,
You have the eyes of a glass serpent.

You taught me how to be Godfather,
Not a father, or a leader.

You taught me how to destroy land,
Not build a ranch, or a reputation.

You think only in percentages,
Yours of course, not ours.

It's no wonder you stink of cancer,
You are rotting from the inside out.

Don't project yourself into me,
I am not your lost pocket mirror.

You shaped yourself through self-debasement,
But I will not lose my edification.

You will never spark cognitive dissonance,
For consensus on your chagrin.

You weighed the cows wrong, admit it,
Your florid three names will not save you now.

Trenchant are the ineligible, who wish
For nothing more than what they work for.

Your resignation was up for reprisal,
But only half-heartedly.

In the end you have saved me,
You have engendered my independence.

You are like a senator who asks a general
To win a war, then banishes him.

Empirically I have judged you
From the throne of my office.

Stop whispering in my ear,
I will not listen anymore.

I would like to name you Rasputin,
Except, you did not succeed.

Philanderer

I saw you entering the home of Tattler in the afternoon
while he was on the other side of the ranch, controlling the harvest.
His wife was inside.
She had asked me earlier for the afternoon off.

Later, when I asked you why, your smiling face gravened, then hardened:
"To get a piece of meat," you said.
What a perfect metaphor!
Yes, you have no fridge in your home,
and the Tattler fridges yours.
Rotund you are,
but you get around well,
red-wine faced and whistling.

And the time I was in town finding tools,
and Tattler's sister was in my kitchen,
the curtains closed,
and when I returned I could not find you in the park:
"On the other side of the house, plucking weeds," you said.

Don't ask me again to errand, ever;
you will hear an excuse, a lie, a truth of All-Knowing.
You will see a face unmirrored, Overlord,
God, tolerant to a fault.

The Warning

Do not call
I will not answer
Not after I warned
Of the flood.

The tractor will not start
And the truck
Will only skate
Over the butter of mud.

Do not laugh
In the rear-view mirror
Of your borrowed truck
While I explain directions.

Gray your hair
And drown in the milky millimeter
Of *vibriosis* vaccination
For the Bulls.

Fifty millimeters
Of rain
Has already fallen
After my warning.

Central Home

Central Home has lights!
It was once Malingerer's home,
Dark and lawned with lemon-tree stumps.

Once it was only called House Twenty-One,
But now the hardest worker lives
There, Tamer of Horses,
Counter, Planter of Trees.

All that is good radiates
From there. Even in the blindness
Of noon. Look! The light has cracked the chimney
And burned the floors!

Misionero, do your *recorridos*,
The count lessening has no excuse.
Do not allow your lot to pass
To overripe clover, do not fall
Into a crack, do not allow
Central Home to become again
House Twenty-One. Let it center the ranch,
Let it be an example.

I have given you electricity,
And fixed your doors.
Misionero, keep it your home.

The Complexity of Managing Ranch Employees

have you found that simple arithmetic
seems like physics,
or does that not bother you anymore,
only bore you, tire you?

have you finally learned to say,
"it's not my fault"?
have you finally learned
that learning is to save yourself?

The Cycle of Things on *Santa Ana* and Everywhere

My new *capataz*,
or should I say my newest,
the one who started working here two years ago
after I fired the bad guys,
has been moving things around—
or should I say acquiring things—
without my permission:
tanks of gas, tools, saddles.
I had a serious talk with him
about the concept of property.

After, as we were walking to the corral
to see the stallions and select which would be kept
and which would be sold and which would become geldings,
I asked him about his family.
He told me his son had quit school
to go to work driving tractors,
and that his daughter
had failed her senior year,
and was working as a teller in a pharmacy.

What a Father Wants to Say to His Son

His son is fourteen,
no longer a boy
and not yet a man.
He does not know what he wants to be,
he knows only that he no longer wants to study,
knows only that he feels restless, bored, fed-up with his place.
He quits school and leaves his mother's house in town
In order to live with his father who is a foreman on a ranch.
He yells, hoots, hollers, laughs when he is on horseback herding the cattle around.
He smiles when he is in the ranch pickup with his father behind the wheel.

While the father and the son drive into town on an errand,
the father notices how his son stares admiringly at the side of his face.
He grits his teeth and tries to smile back,
grips the wheel with forty-five-year-old arthritic hands,
the pain in his left leg (an old injury from falling off a horse) unbearable
every time he steps on the clutch.
He uses a special seat cushion because of his bad back,
and his left eye gums up sometimes,
so he keeps a hankie in his pocket to wipe out the snot.

The father is happy his son chose to come live with him,
happy his son is not out on the streets taking drugs,
breaking in homes, stealing cars.

They drive together, running an errand for *Don*
while *Don* sits in the comfort of his air-conditioned office.
The day is hot and the sun reflects menacingly off the highway.
The only sound is the rubber hissing on the pavement.

It Never Ends

You sit behind your ranch-office desk,
looking at your *capataz* seated in a chair across from you,
a bill for a *carpincho lapicero* that straps to a belt
on the table between you.

Your *capataz* looks and acts like an honest working-class man,
his hair is completely gray at forty-seven,
he wears worn-out clothes,
drives a run-down beat-up car,
volunteers for overtime.

The bill is only for 21 pesos,
but it is a month old
and faxed to you that morning
from a store in town
with the *capataz's* signature on it.

He says he had planned on paying for it before
but had somehow forgotten,
and besides, he told them not to put it on the company account.
Also, he adds, he had paid for it yesterday.

You watch his eyes as he speaks to you
and notice worry.
You think about the good salary you pay him,
the food supplements and clothing you give him,
the rent-free house with electricity and water.
You think about the last few months' bills
that have come across your desk
with inexpensive but questionable items
that you never had time to ask him about.

He leaves your office
and you call one of your secretaries.
You find out he only paid for the *lapicero*
after she asked him what it was for.

You prepare a *mate*,
put it in a backpack,
drive to the edge of Wood
and hike to the center.

You sit upon a fallen tree,
and sip your *mate*.
You hear the soft buzzing of bees around the flowers of a *Paraiso* tree above you.

Moments pass, perhaps more,
then you notice gnats are swarming around a pile of cowshit near your feet,
and, just as you rise to find a different seat,
a silver fox bursts across a clearing in front of you.

In the Local News

Friday, September 7th, 1 A.M.:

It begins to rain heavily,
the sound like barrels of water
being poured on the corrugated roof.

Jonathan locks his office door
and settles into his reading chair
to read a bit and sleep.

Just audible above the sound of water
he hears something else,
like someone rattling
the door handle.

He looks up but the handle is not moving.
Then . . . Bang!
        the door caves convexly in,
shakes on its hinges . . .
Bang. Bang. Bang.

Jonathan is on his feet
in the middle of the room,
an antique branding iron
held in his hand
like a club.

(You see, Jonathan has read often
in the local papers
of similar incidents:
               "In the middle of the night
a rancher robbed and beaten for cash
in his office."
Or,
               "A rancher and his family
robbed at gunpoint in their home
by three ex-convicts hopped up

on meth."

Not that Jonathan couldn't take care of himself, but)

The door bangs and shakes two more times.
Jonathan thinks that his shotgun
might be a better weapon,
and just as he turns to retrieve it,
lightning flashes through the skylights,
blueing the entire office,
his ridiculous shadow twice
on the floor,
and almost simultaneously,
thunder cracks and rumbles away.

Jonathan drops the branding iron,
unlocks and opens the door,

and in leaps
                      Dominic,
   wet
and muddy and panting,
shaking water everywhere.

Dominic never liked thunder.

Another Week Begins

When Jonathan turns off the highway the mud
in the road is a foot deep. He clicks his vehicle
into 4-wheel drive and creeps forward in first gear
so not to slide into one of the ditches. The white gates
of his ranch are open, *Misionero* standing next
to them. He rolls his window down and sighs. The air
smells green. Green. Green.

He drives to his office and talks with his *capataz*,
then they climb in the ranch pickup to go see a calf
cadaver. It was born early that morning with a curled-
neck deformity, and unable to reach its mother's tit
or the water trough, it just stumbled around awhile and fell
on its side. The *gauchos* had skinned it and the vultures picked
it mostly clean, the eyes plucked out, the tongue sliced in half,
bits of intestine lying next to the spine, the heart and lungs mush
under the gristly ribs.

They drive to the Yellow House *casco* to see a pony cadaver.
Apparently, last night it leaped the fence around the
swimming pool and fell in the water. It lay on its side
on the grass where the yardkeeper placed it, its legs
stiff in the curled positions of swimming, yellow froth
tubed out of its nostrils. It was only three-weeks old.

Jonathan goes for a long walk, alone—he admires
the greening grass, the knee-high wheat, the sprouting corn,
the blooming chamomile, the calves and ponies leaping about
pastures spotted white with egrets.

He hears bees buzzing, mockingbirds singing—
and he keeps walking, walking; walking
past the pastures, past Wood,
until he enters a fallow field.

As he approaches a small marsh
a flock of black ibis lift
and cloud away.

Parrot Plague

After working all week
to save the corn crop,

I lie down in the bathtub
        soaking my aching legs,
                contemplating my toes
sticking up out of the water.

I think about the parrot
                I just shot—
      how it fell from the branch
          and too wounded to fly
                began to stumble across the lawn
dragging its wings.

I did not want to waste
another shell,
and I knew a *chimango* would be along
            sooner or later.

While Watching TV After Hunting Opossum all Night

Chickens were missing each morning.
As were eggs.
I had to do something
I did not want to do.

A good movie
with Orson Welles—
Compulsion.

My body betrays my mind.
I will it to move
but it will not.
I finally force it to move
        and it moves in weird
directions,
painfully.

                I ache.

I like maturing,
        acquiring knowledge,
     experiences,
              becoming wiser.

I just don't like
              my body
     giving up on me.

Console me, Wise One, Goddess of Wood—
     tell me Orson—
is this my punishment
            for becoming Hunter?

The Head

I saw a dead body today.
I did not see the head.

I was on my way back from *La Limpieza,*
driving the route Walking Man walks

I was thinking about Advisor, Bad
Guy, Tattler. I was coming around
a dangerous curve, a curve where I have
witnessed the aftermath of many an accident,
skid marks, trucks turned over, logs spilled
onto the road, cars with front ends smashed
in, windshields shattered. Coming around
the curve I slowed down, then stopped
for a white-gloved policeman holding his palm
out. My white truck reflected
in his sunglasses. There was a dark blue
pickup behind him. I waited while the traffic
passed from the other direction. The police
person then waved me forward, his lips and chin gravely
set. I tapped my toe on the accelerator, hoping the cop
would not notice that my seatbelt was unfastened, and drove slowly
past the dark blue pickup. The cab was caved
in, the passenger door open. I saw a man, no,
I saw a body wearing a blue plaid
shirt and blue jeans, the right arm
extended, the hand still gripping
the gear shift. The crushed cab roof
formed a vee that inverted
directly into the middle
of the body's shoulders,
right where the neck should be.
There was no blood, but
I did not see the head.

I saw a dead body today.
I did not see the head.

I was thinking about Advisor, Bad Guy, Tattler.

In the Room of the Dead

Mothballs permeate.

Grandfather slits open
A forty-pound fish
From anus to throat,
His nostrils flaring
At the effluvium.

Grandmother sits upon the lap
Of her gray-suited father,
Her pale dress fluttering
Above her chubby thighs,
Their skin dusted
With corn silk,
Stubble in the field
Behind them.

Your high-headed friend
Who prefers blue oxfords
And khakis with loafers,
Who planted the blooms
That perfume your garden,
Breathes ether and oxygen
Through a plastic mask
And winces at each needle prick
Of the vein-finding nurse.

You mother in lavender chiffon
Who swallowed every morning
whole garlic cloves
Wheezes in a sanitary cloud
Of baby powder,
Her stomach cancer
Taken over.

Your father, a tall man
In a baker's apron,

Sips aromatic *yerba*
In front of a flock
Of sparrows, the birds
scuttling upwind
Of his diabetic
Gangrene feet.

An antique wool blanket
Is folded neatly
Upon the foot of the bed,
And atop the cedar chest of drawers,
The sliver frames
Never quite tarnish to black,
But remain a constant state of gray,

The chromatic faces stilled
By the opening of the door.

Damien Ricardo III and Goneril Elektra

Damien is at the main *tranquera*
with a dozen armed black-suited people behind him,
Goneril is standing beside him
holding a newspaper above her head
to block the sun from her face.
Three grey-suited men with legal pads in their hands
stand to her right.

Damien is Teresa and Obligation's son. Goneril is his wife. Obligation bought this ranch. Obligation died of a heart attack while reading the morning paper some years back. Damien has arrived on the ranch several times over the years trying to push me into a fight. He has ridden our horses to foam when we were lacking broken horses, asked questions about how big the ranch really was, asked why we don't just turn the ranch into all soy, brought friends to the ranch and in front of them tried to order me around like an employee (I just ignored him, which turned him red-faced), used the word usurper behind my back, whispered to his friends loud enough for me to hear that a peon was near while I was cooking asado as a favor, and what I thought of as an obligation for our family. I know if I argue with him in front of his friends (witnesses) it will come to blows and he will have a legal right (with unscrupulous witnesses) to throw me off the ranch or send me to jail. This has all been going on for years. Damien claims to be the owner of the ranch when the county Coyote has a law that states all properties must be shared by the wife and children, or child in this case, fairly until the spouse is dead. Then all properties go to the child. But Damien does not want to wait. He has tried to discredit Teresa's marriage to Obligation, saying it never happened. His wife, who is a lawyer, has powerful friends. Archives in national storage buildings have disappeared. Lawyers and judges who rule in Teresa's favor have mysteriously become ill, resigned, been fired, or died. All I ever did was help Teresa keep this ranch in Obligation's vision, a profitable yet eco-friendly ranch with rivers, streams, lakes, ponds, swamps, wood patches, and feral grasslands mottled among the lots of cows, horses, corn, wheat, and soy. Teresa and I have always planned on turning the idyllic ranch over to Damien and his children someday. I never wanted this job. I just agreed to help Teresa when she asked me. I was a teacher, and I was happy doing that. Possession was never a dream of mine. I am not ambitious. I just have a sense of morality and justice (though these words are temporally and culturally slanted), and an environmentally supportive conscience. I, like Teresa and Obligation (everywhere), want to hear the birds sing, smell fields of flower-spotted wild grasses, wander Wood, hear streams trickle, taste the Salty River in the well water, see foxes, forest cats, armadillos, tegus, opossum, and thousands of other wild fauna and flora exist among the cows, horses, and crops. Damien wants to plow it all under, plant genetically modified soy—which requires an environmentally poisoning pesticide/herbicide to flourish.

A helicopter rises behind Damien and Goneril.
It is black and has a tilted cross painted on
its side. A man in camouflage utilities pushes a body
out of the side door. It lands at my feet. It is not
a body but a mannequin. It looks like me and has a *facón* stuck
in its back.

Let the White Pills,

That were blue before,
And yellow before that,
Slam me into the color
Of sleep.

Two now,
And two before that,
So four before
The wall.

The forgetfulness
Of morning.
Where is the receipt
For the missing
Four-hundred dollars?

Where is the red
Of Hereford,
And the black
Of Angus.

Where are the Fat
Calves
That ghost
The pastures?

Where has Tattler
Parked the pickup
That vacates
The barn?

Morning Routines

breakfast with wife, listen to her as she tells you about the movie she saw the night before, drop the car off at the wash, eat a second breakfast alone, write, go to the office, arrange papers, pick up the jacket and tie at the tailor, pick up the car, find a pocket calculator, see an early movie, alone, spend some time with the grandchildren, relax, talk some more with the wife, organize things for the ranch.

Lie. Lie again. Lie some more. Learn to lie better. Smile. Say good morning even if you don't want to. Tell them anything, but don't tell the truth. "The *varillas* were mismade," not, "I didn't have time to pick them up, I was drunk the night before." Get them working. Say you'll arrive tomorrow. They lie, worse. They lie to steal. You lie for the good, for truth. Get up early, pack a sandwich, a thermos of coffee, a *mate*, two bottles of water, a duffle bag with a change of clothes, a shaving kit, shower shoes to prevent foot fungus while using the cheap hotel shower where you wait as an insomniac so you can arrive the next morning and surprise them and see if they are really working during the hours set, check the dead cows and see if the carcasses are fresh, check the fenceline, count the meters. There is no one except your wife that you can trust. She is the only good in your life. They, they all lie, cheat, steal. Be badder than they are for the good. Be bad. Be a son-of-a-bitch. Thou shalt not lie. Thou shall not lie. Thou shall not lie. Did god lie to us? Did Henry the Fifth lie to get his wife, who was rightfully not or not his? Is a person property? Land? A ranch? It is all so temporal. We must give back to maintain the balance. Plant some trees. Let a field fallow. Leave another as marsh. Arrive at the ranch. Check the kilometers on the truck. Give the dogs some meat. Check the medications in the barn. Don't go the office and check the messages, go to the ranchhouse, lock the door, and open a bottle of wine.

breakfast with wife, listen to her as she tells you about the movie she saw the night before, drop the car off at the wash, eat a second breakfast alone, write, go to the office, arrange papers, pick up the jacket and tie at the tailor, pick up the car, find a pocket calculator, see an early movie, alone, spend some time with the grandchildren, relax, talk some more with the wife, organize things for the ranch.

His Nightly Bottle of Wine

Seven wine bottles a weekend
The smiling gaucho, Whistling
Gaucho pitches in the trash hole.

My problem with your numbers
Is not my problem with your numbers
But my problems with my numbers.

Achilles and Hector both drank
Cups of wine each night
And made love to their wo-men,

As did every foot soldier
Who could, or should, or would
Leave their battle-mates' tents.

My brother is the spider, the fox,
The armadillo; my cousin is mathematics;
My family flamingoes over the river.

Stop searching through my trash,
My briefcase, my pockets; stop
Investigating my office corners.

Whistler broke the tractor
By running over a tree stump
Then crashing through an electric fence.

Tattler, cut the thistle
While it still is in bloom,
Don't tale me fence repair.

My charts are not updated
Though even in the spring
You short cows grass.

My nightly bottle of wine

Helped me to forget
That tomorrow is not an end,

That family is a temporal term,
That loyalty is leaving, that wrath
Has no place in eternity.

Communication with the Capataz

I have yet to speak your tongue,
To communicate well with you.
I tire when you talk,
Anger at my vocabulary.

The universal language is explanation,
Not repetition.

Sit, sit; Sit! teacher of diction
And tell me what you came to say.
Don't translate,
It only makes matters worse.

What substance are words?
They are not the thing.
A tree is an *árbol,*
Yet it is a thing
That grows and branches,
Buds, leaves, flowers, fruits,
Falls.
A tree decomposes,
Enriches the soil for other trees,
Becomes a part of other trees.
Leave the tree to it.
It is it.

A cow calves many times
And then it dies.
Her calves calve.
They die.

Language births, grows, expands, replicates;
Nouns verb,
Then the tongue incorporates,
Enriches another,
Seems at times to vanish,
Yet,

The root remains.

The thing that was,
Is.

Don't tell me the tree,
Show me.

Place for the Pueblo Teacher

You enter the café like a Greek
Statue, pliable by movement,
Flawed only by pimples.

Do you really want to lose
Your virginity to the man
With sunlight in his eyes?

Twenty-nine to two-fifteen
To two-ten. The rain clouds
My corneas, my vision of you.

Marriage is too much
For the man who prefers to drive
The side roads rather than
The expressway, even with
Your beauty, your wit.

All roads lead into town:
It is impossible to be lost
Here, unless you take a detour.

When I am in the city,
I remember why I escape
To the ranch. When I am
On the ranch, I remember why
I want to live in the city.

You are not for this town,
Your country eyes do not shine
Like streetlamps.

Do not go to live where
Your father came from; go
Only to visit, wander the streets.

The Language Teacher

Whip me with commands,
Correct my grammar, curl
My tongue and flick it against
The roof of my mouth. Paddle
Me with your cruel consonants, laugh,
Point with your soft finger
To the shine on your high vowels,
To the highlighted phrase.

Do not chase the man
In the internet chat room,
He may take you to an unlit alley at night.

Your Violet Hair Ribbon

Last night you slept with your head on my chest,
My nose in your hair.

While I dozed the violet ribbon upon my wrist
Broke and fell off. This morning I searched for it
But could not find it, anywhere. I tied a new one
To my ankle. Hid another in my journal cover.

Did you have the same dream I did last night?
You with your head on your husband's chest,
My wife with hers on mine.

Teresa: My Mask of Day

My mask of day rises with me out of bed
like a wrapped sheet: clinging, covering, she hides
the scars of night; she is soft, sensuous, caresses
my muscular build, my face, my hair;

She unwraps and pirouettes before me, holds out her arms,
clasps my hand, ballrooms, tangos:
She jumps up and down upon the dry earth,
raising dust to form a rain cloud.

She does not resee my nightmares,
or remember them for me upon wakening.
She does not see the half-bottle of scotch
I sipped into my veins the night before.

She grinds coffee and pours spring water through
the grounds, serves me in a porcelain cup.
She scrambles eggs and sets the plate
before me. She does not ask

Where I was the afternoon before,
or who I was with. She sits in the chair
next to mine, places her hand upon
my forearm, and says nothing.

Teresa: Translator

You are the translator of my day.
I fall into your graphite eyes
When we transmute,
I find your hands
The hands of a maker:
Soft and crafting.
I want to caress the curve
Of your lip,
Speak to your breasts.
Become my left ear
And I shall remain my right—
Where we meet we will middle.
The spider feasts
In the web of my thoughts,
And pastures modern
The corners of your culture—
Remove the weeds
Of your socialization.
Idiom me,
Invite me into the woods of your words,
Seat me at your banquet table.
You are the coffee of my mornings,
The *mate* of my afternoons.
Why do you hide your syllables
Under your tongue?
Don't you ever question
The power of words,
The meaning of sleep?
Yes, I know you do,
In nightmares—
And in this I second your revival.
The grass grows at night,
And in the heat of mosquitoes,
So let the wildflowers grow.
Language me inside Wood,
Ranch me where the city
Has not yet encroached.

Marsh me where the ranch cannot reach.
You are the queen of my kingdom,
That I have so temporally created.
You are the singer of my verse.
Interpret my dreams.

On a Winter Walk

"Garner some violets,"
Teresa said to me.
"They are perceptually constant,
Under the trees."

Transition

When the cows have eaten all the grass
And the butcher cannot buy,
What do we do with the clover
That has not yet recovered?

When the bulls leap barbwire
To find the cows in heat,
What do we do with the toothless
Hags tagging behind their calves?

When the sheep return to Twenty-One
And the shepherd is on the highway,
What do we do with the fallen twigs
And the uncut park grass?

When the fenceposts lie to rot in ponds
And Fencer curves his line,
What do we do with the logger truck
Lumber Jack false-bottomed?

When Counter cannot count
And the horse herd shrinks while growing,
What do we do with the unlearned leader
That has yet to earn his office?

When the land transforms from marsh to wheat
And Seeder sprays more herbicide,
What do we do for the migrating ducks
And the butterflies missed by bankers?

The Salty River

I was standing on a grassy hill
overlooking the Salty River
that winds and flows
along *Santa Ana*'s north-western border.
The sun was about to set
and the star was turning orange.
The Ponies and Calves were leaping about
as if celebrating the survival of another day.
The corn was knee high, and the wheat fields
were shorn to short stalks that looked
like the three-day blond stubble of a recently shaped beard.
Birds were chirping and singing
like they too were reveling in the End.
The Cultivators were nowhere to be seen,
their noxious machinery fumes and pesticides
not clouding the air or poisoning the Earth.
The *Gauchos* were all in their homes
with their families, eating, or drinking *mate*.

Just as the sun disappeared over the horizon,
The Pink Flamingoes in the river hued red.

Ennui

Old Man

On my weekly drives
to *La Limpieza*,
I sometimes see Old Man
walking on the shoulder
of the road.
He is gray-bearded,
and calvitied. He wears
a tattered black suit.
He lugs a filthy sheet
knapsack upon his
back. He never thumbs,
nor pleads for a ride
with his sun-bleached eyes.
He walks slowly, determinedly,
much slower of course
than the cars and trucks
that blow by inches
from his shoulder.
I never see him stopped,
sitting down, or drinking
coffee in a truck stop.
He is always walking,
always walking.

Glossary

árbol: Tree

asado: 1. An outside grill for cooking meat. 2. Cooking style on an outside grill using coals or wood fire.

bombilla: Variation of straw, or tube. Made of metal, wood, or bamboo. Used for drinking *mate* out of a gourd.

capataz: Foreman

carpincho: A large aquatic rodent, about the size of a medium-sized dog. Pelt when removed of hair is suede-like, and used to make jackets, hats, shoes belts, key chains, etc.

casco: The area or lot of land the main house on the ranch occupies. A large yard.

cordero: Lamb.

chimango: A type of hawk. A beautifully luteous one, which, like most hawks, eats serpents, rodents, pigeons, and carrion. It also has a mischievous side, (one that has caused Argentine naturalists to call it "dishonorable") as it is known to rob eggs and hatchlings from other *genus avis*.

Dominic: From the late Latin name *Dominicus* meaning "of the Lord". This name was traditionally given to a child or animal born on Sunday.

Don: Boss or owner of ranch. Also used as a salutation of respect.

escribiano: Notary public.

estancia: Ranch.

facón: A sharp knife carried on the belts of gauchos. Used to skin dead cows before the hide hardens and is useless. Gauchos use them in knife fights or pull them out and begin sharpening them when they feel threatened or are trying to threaten you.

facturas: Sweet rolls.

gaucho: Argentine cowboy. Ranch worker.

La Limpieza: The second fictional ranch in this book.

lapicero: A braided leather keyring chain that connects a keyring to a beltloop. More elaborate ones have silver and/or gold rings on them.

mate: A loose-leaf tea. The dried and pulverized leaves of the *Yerba* tree are poured into a gourd, then a metal straw called a *bombilla* with a filtering device on one end is plunged in. Hot water is poured over the leaves and the liquid mixture is sipped through the *bombilla.* It is pleasantly bitter, and is the Argentine national drink. There is a whole culture and many customs that are sociologically intriguing for preparing and sharing *mate,* e.g., it is a sign of love, friendship, and/or respect when more than one person shares the same *mate;* who in the group prepares the mate; who pours the water, and which direction the *mate* is passed; when to accept and decline a drink. If you stumble upon a group of people drinking *mate,* or you go to someone's house and the he/she does not offer you *mate,* that is a strong signal that they do not want you to stick around. The amount of times per day *mate* is drunk correlates with social status and self-image. *Mate* is usually drunk in the early morning because it is a stimulant, and at the end of the work day because it is a restorative, but workers who have access to it drink it all day long. Unbeknown to most people who do drink it, it contains vitamin C, phosphorous, and chlorophyll that combine to promote disease resistance, cellular activity, digestive processes, and arbitrarily prevent people who live on mostly meat diets from contracting scurvy.

matera: Place where employees take *mate* breaks.

Misionero: A person born in Misiones, Argentina

Pampas: Argentina's Plains, or grasslands. Perfect for cattle grazing or turning into a farm, as no tree cutting is needed. All of the trees, forests, and woodlands on the *Pampas* were planted, or at least started, centuries ago by early European settlers. Now, unfortunately, big-money profit-seeking business people are trying to buy up all the *Pampas,* cut down all the trees, drain the swamps and lakes, raze the houses, then plant genetically modified soy—which requires an environmentally-poisoning herbicide/pesticide to flourish (which Jonathan is trying to prevent in this book).

peón: Ranch worker, not necessarily derogatory in Spanish.

pueblo: A small town (noun). In one case in this book, it is used as a verb.

rastra: an elaborate belt buckle worn by *gauchos*.

recorrido: A circular route. A tour. In this case: a daily horseback tour of the ranch. During a *recorrido*, a *gaucho* checks on the health of the animals, the state of grass, water, and general security.

Santa Ana: A fictitious ranch that lies next to the fictitious Salty River. The main locale in the book.

señor: Sir. Mister. Boss. Pronoun or title used as a sign of respect.

Tegu: a large black-and-white lizard almost as big as Gila Monster.

ternero: Cow calf.

tranquera: Wooden gate, used as an entrance to a ranch and divider between lots of land.

varillas: Rectangular or square-shaped wooden rods with holes drilled through them to allow the fenceline to pass through, and are placed about a meter apart between fence posts to keep the fenceline straight and taut and prevent the animals from escaping by pushing their bodies through the fenceline between posts.

vibriosis: STD that sterilizes bulls and causes cows to abort.

yerba: Variation of the word *hierba*, or herb. A loose-leaf tea also called *yerba-mate*. Made from the leaves of the *Yerba* tree.

yerba tree: Of the evergreen oak family but about the size of a small pear tree.

yerra: A yearly job on a ranch where the *gauchos* turn young male calves into steers. It is quite a cowboy show (now considered barbaric), with the corral filled with the male calves, and the gauchos (holding lassoes) lined in a gauntlet outside. Then, the calves are released one by one, and made to run the gauntlet with lassoes flying out at it. When one of the *gauchos* successfully lassoes a calf, it is then wrestled to the ground, a *facón* appears, and the calf is castrated. The wound is then sterilized with a mixture of disinfectants, and the calf is released to wobble in the direction of the herd. After all the calves are gelded, the atmosphere becomes festive—a fat cow is slaughtered and the ranch's owners, family, friends, neighbors, staff, and *gauchos* feast and drink wine.

References

Assuncao, Fernando. *The Mate*. Buenos Aires: Mar y Sol ediciones, 2001.

Assuncao, Fernando O. *Historia del Gaucho* (History of the Gaucho). Buenos Aires: Editorial Claridad S.A., 1999.

Baretto, Margarita. *El Mate* (the Mate). Buenos Aires: Ediciones del Sol, 1998.

Biloni, José Santos. *Arboles Argentinos* (Argentine Trees). Buenos Aires: Tipográfica Editora Argentina, 1990.

Caneveri, Marcelo, Carlos Fernández Balboa. *100 Mamíferos Argentinas* (100 Argentine Mammals). Buenos Aires: Albatross, 2003.

Caneveri, Pablo, Tito Nrosky. *Cien Aves Argentinas* (One Hundred Argentine Birds). Buenos Aires: Albatross, 1995.

Carrere, Ricardo. *Monte Indígena* (Indigenous Woods). Buenos Aires: Editorial Nordan-comunidad, 2001.

Cinti, Roberto Rainer. *Fauna Argentina* (Argentine Fauna). Buenos Aires: Emecé, 2005.

Comte, Mónica G. Hoss de la. *The Gaucho*. Buenos Aires: Ediciones Maizal, 1999.

Comte, Mónica G. Hoss de la. *The Mate*. Buenos Aires: Ediciones Maizal, 1999.

Comte, Mónica G. Hoss de la. *The Tango*. Buenos Aires: Ediciones Maizal, 1999.

Dowdall, Carlos R. *Criollo el Caballo del Pais* (Argentine horse Breeds). Buenos Aires: Vazquez Mazzini Editores, 2003.

Espíndola, Athos. *Diccionario del Lunfardo* (Argentine Slang Dictionary). Buenos Aires: Planeta, 2002.
Figueroa, Luis. *El Gaucho* (The Gaucho). Buenos Aires: Buenos Aires: Ediciones Casa Figueroa, 1999.

Gobello, José. *Diccionario Gauchesco* (Gaucho Dictionary). Buenos Aires: Editorial Dunken, 2003.

Haene, Eduardo, Gustavo Aparicio. *100 Árboles*. Buenos Aires: Albatross, 2001.

Narosky, T., D. Yzurieta. *Aves de Argentina y Uruguay* (Birds of Argentina and Uruguay). Buenos Aires: Vazquez Mazzini Editores, 1993.

Petretti, Francesco. *Aves* (Birds). Barcelona: Grijalbo, 1978.

Rock, David. *Argentina 1516-1987: From Spanish Colonization to Alfonsín*. Los Angeles: University of California Press, 1987.

Saubidet, Tito. *Vocabulario y Refranero Criollo* (Argentine Vocabulary). Buenos Aires: Letemendia Casa Editora, 2002.

Schuster, Simon and. *Simon and Schuster's International Dictionary: English/Spanish, Spanish/English*. New York: Simon and Schuster: 1978.

Sundstrom, Harold W., Mary O. Sundstrom. *Collies*. New York: Barrows, 1994.

Vega, Santiago G. de la. *Iguazú: The Laws of the Jungle*. Buenos Aires: Contacto Silvestre Ediciones, 2003.

Vega, Santiago G. de la. *Patagonia: The Laws of the Forest*. Buenos Aires: Contacto Silvestre Ediciones, 2003.

Acknowledgements

The following poems have been published:

"Jonathan Goes to Search for It at Sunset": *vox poetica* and anthologized in a different version in *Voice & Verse Magazine*
"Muse in Different Forms": *Fox Chase Review*
"Ally, AKA Advisor, Resigns," "Fauna," and "Teresa: Translator": *North of Oxford*
"Finally": *Zymbol*
"Dear Father": *Foliate Oak Literary Magazine*
"The Salty River," "Cattle Rustler," "Satellites," "The Head," "In the Local News," "Damien Ricardo III and Goneril Electra," "Your Violet Hair Ribbon," "Another Week Begins": *madswirl*
"Horse Thief": *Cascadia Review*
"Bad Guy Caught Red Handed": *Western Press Books—Manifest West*
"Tattler," "Casca and Tattler," "Tattler's Reindoctrination": *Poetry Pacific*
"His Name is Pac-Man": *Hinchas de Poesia*
"On a Breath-Mist Morning": *Bennington Review*
"Last Night I Dreamed Rain," and "On Ranching": *Two Hawks Quarterly*
"The Wayward," and *"Misionero"*: *Renovation Journal*
"Teresa: My Mask of Day": *Santa Fe Literary Review*
"Punch Clock": *The New Plains Review*
"The King of Clear": *Reunion - The Dallas Review*
"The Legend of Wood" and "Central Home": *Excavating the Underground*
"The Complexity of Managing Ranch Employees," and "On a Winter Walk": *SouthFlorida Arts Journal*
"The Cycle of Things on Santa Ana and Everywhere": *The Paddock Review*
"Excuse Maker," and "What a Father Wants to Say to his Son": *Red Dashboard LLC, Unbridled*
"It Never Ends": *Hobo Camp Review*
"Transition," "Old Man": *Lit Up Magazine*
"In the Room of the Dead": *Bravura Literary Journal (won the 2019 First Place Prize for Poetry)*

My thanks to Megan Albert, Amanda Auchter, CB, Ethel Louise Beach, Brittney Beauregard, Nancy Beauregard, John Belcher, Ángel Beltramino, Lara Berman, April Bernard, Sven Birkets, Butch Blaesing, Rachel Blumenfeld, Gene and Flossie Brill, Michael Burkard, JC; James Cervantes, Elaine F. Chapman, Susan

Cheever, Sandra Cisneros, Lynn Clanton, Victoria Clausi, MH Clay, Susan Deer Cloud, Kevin Cooper, Mikael Covey, Deb and John Cox, Esther Cross, Franco and Mariela Cuevas, Yago S. Cura, Jeffery DeLargy, Jim Daniels, Dawn Dayton, Laura Dinovis, Athena Dixon, David Drake, Doug and Mary Drake, Michael Dumanis, Kelly Dumar, Nicole Dunas, James H Duncan, Anna Evans, Elizabeth Farrell, David Figueroa, Athena Fliakos, Ross Furgeson, Diane Sahms-Guarnieri, Marguerite Feitlowitz, Rodger French, Cheyenne Gallion, Amy Gerstler, Lynn Gobeille, Annabel Davis-Goff, Diane Sahms-Guarnieri, Garrett Dennert, Kate Hanson, William Harry Harding, ML Harrison, Ben Hartlage, Kimberly Hawlena, Stephen Moria Hawk, Eddie Two Hawks, Sean Heaney, Jim Heavily, Carol Heeb, Dee and Don Henderson, Heather Shellnut Hillary, Laurie Higi, Janice Kaminski Hitzing, Colette Inez, Major Jackson, Anne James, Rhiannon James, Kevin and Ronnie Gennette-Jazowski, Dr. J, Mark Jenkins, Dana M. John, Anne Johnson, Angela Kaiser, Nancy Kaminski, Kathy Kazuma, Christen Kincaid, Ryan Kincaid, Kathleen King, Susan Kinsolving, Margaret Kolasa, Dave and Mary Kraft, Megan Kraft, Patricia Padovini-Krause, Tammy Ho Lai-Ming, Mong-Lan, Angela Boer Lannes, Lara Boer Lannes, Rustin Larson, Ruth Larson, Erica Plouffe Lazure, Ann Leamon, Bianca Lech, Jamie LeMasters, Akiko Lemoine, Patrick Lemoine, Sanaë Lemoine, Woody Lewis, Timothy Liu, Chip Livingston, Annmarie Lockhart, Michael Long, Deborah A. Lott, Amy MacLennan, Stacey Magner, Elizabeth Maines, Kevin Maines, Leah Maines, Caroline Malone, Tyler Malone, Becca Mannery, Geraldine Marcs, Milana Marsenich, Carlos Martinez, Kate McCahill, Shay McCleavy, Rebecca McCorry, Leslie McGrath, James McKenna, David Meischen, Askold Melnyczuk, Susan Merrell, Donigan Merritt, Jalina Mhyana, Teresa Milbrodt, Jenn Monroe, Joe Morrison, Alfredo Mueller, Jeannie Murphy, Holly Murten, Lauren Myers, Vi Khi Nao, Allene Nichols, Ken Nichols, Lyle Nichols, Rachel Nix, Jules Nyquist, Ed Ochester, Caley O'Dwyer, Akiko Okuma, Johnny Olson, Madelyn Olson, Caitlin O'Neil-Amaral, Martin Ott, Gerald and Margaret Page, Maryann Page, Rod Page, Carolina Papaleo, Osvaldo Papaleo, Lidia Papaleo, Cheryl Pappas, Kimberly Parko, Catherine Parnell, Jeffery Perkins, Katie Perkins, Nélida Pessagno, Kimberly Peterson, Sam Philbeck, Yolanda Pitaluga, Marc duPlan, Fabrice B. Poussin, Gardner Powell, Amanda Preston, Ramón Puerta, Liam Rector, Katie Rauk, Alicia Referda, g emil reutter, Isabel Roche, Emilia Robles, Salina Rodriguez, Armand Rosamilia, Raye Rose, Claire Rosenzweig, Lauren Sapala, Carolyn Welch Scarborough, Dr. Terry Schliesman, David Scronce, Diane Shaffer, Leslie T. Sharpe, Bonnie Shellnut, Mariko

Silver, Sandra Simonds, Marissa Sinisi, Savannah Sloan, Bailey Smith, Sarah Sousa, Bailey Spry, Shawn Shellnut Spry, Cornelia (Nell) Stanton, Elizabeth A. Stelling, Bob Swanson, Lynn Swanson, Andre Tan, Neil Tesh, David Thane, Jennifer Therieau, Mrs. Thompson, Ani Torres, Erin Trahan, Cheryl Tucker, Joshua Tyler, Peggy C. Turnull, J Todd Underhill, Alejandro Vacarro, Sarah Valente, Jakob VanLammeren, Sandra Vazquez, Joyce Whitaker Hall-Wakeman, Michael Waggoner, Theresa and Mike Kaminski Williams, Zavia Willis, Jennifer Winebrenner, Mrs. Wines, Scott Wiggerman, Ray Windsor, Mark Wunderluch, Kimberly Young, Changming Yuan, Michael Yuan, Yesha, Marcos Zapiola, and Alan Ziegler.

Stephen Page part Apache and Shawnee. He was born in Detroit. He is the author of three other books of poetry—*A Ranch Bordering the Salty River, The Timbre of Sand,* and *Still Dandelions*. He holds two AA's from Palomar College, a BA from Columbia University, and an MFA from Bennington College. He also attended Broward College. His literary criticisms have appeared regularly in the *Buenos Aires Herald, How Journal, Gently Read Literature, North of Oxford,* and the *Fox Chase Review*. His short stories have been published in *Quarto, The Whistling Fire, Amphibi, Bold + Italic* and *Mad Swirl*. His haiku and senryu have appeared in *Frogpond, Hedgerow, brass bell, Black Bough, Bravura, Brussels Sprout, Cicada, Haiku Headlines, Heron Quarterly, Japanophile, Our Reader's Quarterly, Piedmont Literary Review,* and *Point Judith Light*. He is the recipient of The Jess Cloud Memorial Prize, a Writer-in-Residence from the Montana Artists Refuge, a Full Fellowship from the Vermont Studio Center, an Imagination Grant from Cleveland State University, and an Arvon Foundation Ltd. Grant. He loves long walks through woodlands, communing with nature, reading, spontaneous road trips, his wife, family, friends, dog-earing books, throwing cellphones into lakes, and making noise with his Fender Precision bass.

Additional Praise for *The Salty River Bleeds*

The Salty River Bleeds is equal parts parable and fable, examining humankind's destructive and self-defeating tendencies, particularly with regard to caring for the land human beings and animals rely on. Here where the Salty River bleeds, you will find that Myth swims, Old Man lingers on your peripheral vision only to disappear, and Black Dog follows you into the mythic Wood. On the ranch, you will encounter Tattler, Excuse Maker, and Bad Guy, archetypal figures standing in for all those whose motives are to be questioned. By turns imaginative and inventive, gritty and grisly, gorgeous and ephemeral, this is a book that will linger long after you have finished. There are inherent truths laid bare here that we would all do well to pay heed.
 —**Cati Porter**, author of *Seven Floors Up*

In Stephen Page's *The Salty River Bleeds*, the spiritual journey of Jonathan continues from A Ranch Bordering the Salty River. Looking for a story to explain his life, Jonathan meditates on nature, in particular Wood, a place of testing, a place of mysteries ripe to be discovered, and the people who work his land without reverence. With an observant eye for detail, Page brings together striking images of the elements of earth and human life that become both obstacles to and medium through which the speaker of these poems understands his world.
 —**Caroline Malone**, author of *Dark Roots*

Stephen Page's *The Salty River Bleeds* is a pastoral and violent account of ranch life. His poetic collection blends agricultural and rustic contention with eco-rural insight and directness. His delivery is candid and un-floral, thus bestowing the music of his perception an energy of seized quotidian acuity. These poems dare the readers to care about the animals, the daily activities of surviving rurally, and the grammar of the land exploited by genetic modified commerce and industrialization. The work invites the geography of natural breeding life to marry the perennial charm of ranch hardship. There, in his work, exists the sensual preservation of humanity, but also diurnal desires. Page's bucolic poems "may take you to an unlit alley at night" or "sound like buckets of water being poured on the corrugated roof." Regardless of the rustic tempo his work imbues you, through Page's percipient, omniscient eyes, we see and hear everything he observes and feels and yearns. Like sheep hides "salted in the transit room"—Page's work is designed to ambush us, not with the forcefulness or melancholy of existence, but, as seen here, with the authoritative authenticity

of his persistent fervor.
—**Vi Khi Nao**, author of *Fish in Exile*

Stephen Page's *The Salty River Bleeds* is a collection of connections. Page explores relationships, ethics, and economy through environmental images that ooze the intricacies of farm life. His thoughtful, sensory-rich prose and varied expressions of poetic form delve into the inner workings of losses and discoveries.
—**Savannah Slone**, Author of *Hearing the Underwater*

Stephen Page is a true poetic chronicler of the complex business of ranching, that mythic journey. *The Salty River Bleeds* is iconic storytelling; a hybrid of poems, letters, and prose. Filled with rich images, "wood walks" and myth finding. "Life takes you into some unplanned territory." Follow Page and we are "wading into wheat" and "working all week to save the corn." The tractor is broken, the fences need mending, but still we are watching and waiting for Old Man walking by the side of the road, the one who never stops. Follow Page into his dreamscape of visceral reality to satisfy a curiosity, an unspoken desire.
—**Elaine Fletcher Chapman**, author of Hunger for Salt

In *The Salty River Bleeds*, Stephen Page poetically and unapologetically reveals the real, harsh truths of running a ranch in Argentina. Johnathan's daily stressors, created by unreliable employees, weather, and Teresa's greedy son, Damien, find us anxiously watching him "run across pastures with my sword / Raised, looking for someone to decapitate." Page softens Johnathan's persona by peppering the pages with love, beauty, mate, and the whimsy of Wood and Myth as "A wooddove pops / its wings as it departs eucalypti mist auraed by / a vanilla sunrise." The juxtaposition of the hard and the soft leaves us with a longing to know how Jonathan and Teresa's story ends. The Fauna of this collection proves to be a mesmerizing sequel to the Flora of the initial introduction of Johnathan and Teresa in his earlier collection, *A Ranch Bordering the Salty River.*
—**Laurie Higi**, author of *The Universe of Little Beaver Lake*

CPSIA information can be obtained
at www.ICGtesting.com
Printed in the USA
FSHW011501220919
62240FS

9 781646 620258